Put Beginning Readers on the Right Track with
ALL ABOARD READING™

The All Aboard Reading series is especially designed for beginning readers. Written by noted authors and illustrated in full color, these are books that children really want to read—books to excite their imagination, expand their interests, make them laugh, and support their feelings. With fiction and nonfiction stories that are high interest and curriculum-related, All Aboard Reading books offer something for every young reader. And with four different reading levels, the All Aboard Reading series lets you choose which books are most appropriate for your children and their growing abilities.

Picture Readers
Picture Readers have super-simple texts, with many nouns appearing as rebus pictures. At the end of each book are 24 flash cards—on one side is a rebus picture; on the other side is the written-out word.

Station Stop 1
Station Stop 1 books are best for children who have just begun to read. Simple words and big type make these early reading experiences more comfortable. Picture clues help children to figure out the words on the page. Lots of repetition throughout the text helps children to predict the next word or phrase—an essential step in developing word recognition.

Station Stop 2
Station Stop 2 books are written specifically for children who are reading with help. Short sentences make it easier for early readers to understand what they are reading. Simple plots and simple dialogue help children with reading comprehension.

Station Stop 3
Station Stop 3 books are perfect for children who are reading alone. With longer text and harder words, these books appeal to children who have mastered basic reading skills. More complex stories captivate children who are ready for more challenging books.

In addition to All Aboard Reading books, look for All Aboard Math Readers™ (fiction stories that teach math concepts children are learning in school) and All Aboard Science Readers™ (nonfiction books that explore the most fascinating science topics in age-appropriate language).

All Aboard for happy reading!

For Wendy Hashmall
with many thanks—N.K.

Photo credits: Front cover, pages 8, 41: © Getty Images Allsport USA ; title page, back cover, pages 5, 11, 15, 24, 27, 30, 34, 37, 42, 45: © AP/Wide World Photos; pages 7, 20, 33, 46: © 2002 Newsday, Inc.; p 19: © Leah Adams.

Library of Congress Cataloging-in-Publication Data is available.

ISBN   0-448-43102-5 (pbk.)   A   B   C   D   E   F   G   H   I   J
ISBN   0-448-43103-3 (GB)   A   B   C   D   E   F   G   H   I   J

SARAH HUGHES

GOLDEN GIRL

By Nancy Krulik
with photographs

Grosset & Dunlap • New York

"The Best I've Ever Done!"

Sixteen-year-old Sarah Hughes seemed to be floating as she skated across the ice. Her smile was bright. Her jumps were high, clean, and crisp. Her lavender dress sparkled under the lights in the Salt Lake Ice Center. One TV broadcaster said watching Sarah skate was like seeing Tinkerbell fly.

Sarah had completed her short program and began the long program in fourth place. It would take a flawless

performance to go from fourth to first. But Sarah had nothing to lose. She just had to go out there and skate her best.

Sarah's best was *amazing*. She'd planned the hardest long program of all the skaters, with two triple-triple combination jumps. That was something no woman had ever landed in an Olympic competition.

Sarah leaped into the air. Triple Salchow-triple loop combination. Triple toe-triple loop.

"Oh my gosh!" the announcer shouted. "That's four triples in less than one and a half minutes."

Sarah kept going. Once again she leaped into the air. Another triple-triple combination!

PERFECT.

Sarah Hughes during her long program at the Salt Lake
Ice Center

"This is the kind of performance you just dream about!" the sportscaster shouted.

As the music came to an end, hundreds of flowers and stuffed animals showered down on the ice. Sarah's coach, Robin Wagner, grabbed her by the shoulders. "Close your eyes. Take a deep breath," Robin told her. "Now open your

Sarah with one of the stuffed animals she received after skating her long program

eyes. I want you to remember this moment forever."

Sarah had skated the best she ever

had. But would it be good enough to earn her the gold?

Only time would tell.

Sarah had been the first of the top four skaters to perform her long program. Other competitors would be going for the gold as well, including more experienced skaters Michelle Kwan and Irina Slutskaya.

All Sarah could do was wait.

Finally, the last skater, Russia's Irina Slutskaya, finished her program. Irina's scores flashed on the screen. But a camera was also on Sarah, who was waiting back-stage. The NBC cameraman did some fast math. According to his figuring, Sarah Hughes had just won the gold medal.

As the cameraman whispered the news to Sarah, her eyes opened wide. At first she didn't say anything. Then she and her coach let out huge screams. Sarah dropped to the floor. She couldn't believe it. She was the Olympic gold medalist!

Later, as Sarah felt the heavy gold medal being slipped around her neck at the awards ceremony, she looked at the crowd. She watched the American flag being raised. She listened to "The Star-Spangled Banner" being played in the arena. She heard the crowd cheering for her. She was an Olympic gold medalist! Sarah would remember this moment forever.

It was the moment she'd dreamed of her whole life, ever since she'd laced up her very first pair of skates.

A N-ice Kid!

Sarah Elizabeth Hughes was born May 2, 1985, in Great Neck, New York, a suburb of New York City. Her arrival was cheered by her parents Amy and John, as well as her older sister Rebecca and big brothers Matt and David. (Younger sisters Emily and Taylor would come along a few years later.)

Sarah's dad was born in Canada, a country where skating is a very big deal. John Hughes had been captain of a national championship hockey team at Cornell University. He wanted his kids to love skating, too.

The first time Sarah skated, she was only three years old. Sarah's mother was really surprised when Sarah started to skate all by herself! But she needn't have worried. Sarah was a natural from the very start.

Sarah was the last one in the family to have her skates tied. She had to wait until the older kids were ready before she could skate. Sarah didn't like that one bit. So she learned to lace her own skates.

At three, Sarah was tying her own skates. By five she'd learned how to do Axel jumps, double Salchows, and double toe loops. She'd also learned to play games on the ice.

"I don't remember the first time I

skated," Sarah told New York's *Newsday*. "I remember being really young and taking group skating. We played red light, green light. The instructor was at one end, and whoever reached the other end first, won."

Sarah didn't just skate at nearby rinks. She had a skating rink in her own backyard! Sarah's dad had the rink built so that he and his kids could skate and play ice hockey right at home.

But Sarah didn't get to do a whole lot of practicing on that home rink. Her older brothers liked to organize neighborhood hockey games. She had to battle the bigger guys for ice time.

By the time Sarah was six, she was performing in local ice shows, including one at New York City's famous Rockefeller Center. That same year, Sarah was invited to take part in a show in Lake Placid, New York. Also skating in that show was Kristi Yamaguchi. Kristi had just won the 1992 Olympic gold medal. She was one of Sarah's heroes, along with other Olympic champs Scott Hamilton and Peggy Fleming.

Scott Hamilton and Peggy Fleming at the opening ceremonies of the 2002 Winter Games

Sarah hadn't even finished second grade and she was already skating in the same show with a gold medalist. No doubt about it, this little girl was on her way to something big.

"I Want to do That!"

One afternoon, Sarah and some other third graders were taking a lesson at the local rink on Long Island. A coach named Robin Wagner just happened to be there. Of all the kids in the rink, it was Sarah who caught Robin's eye.

"The joy in her face, the twinkle in her eye," Robin explained to a reporter for the *Kansas City Star*. "There is just a joy in being out on the ice. She'd fall down and get back up, and fall down and get up. You don't see many people with that much enthusiasm."

Sarah had what it took. Robin was sure of it. She began working with the young skater. Before long, Sarah found herself in France, touring with Olympic skaters Surya Bonaly and Alexander Zhulin.

"When I saw the Olympic skaters, I thought, 'I want to do that,'" she told *People* magazine.

And Sarah *would* someday be an Olympic skater. But there was a lot of work to be done before that could happen. For starters, Sarah would have to practice many more hours each day—while still going to school. That meant skating before and after classes.

Sarah also had to do a lot of traveling.

The rink she'd been taking lessons on in Long Island wasn't right for serious training. Robin knew of another rink, the Ice House, in Hackensack, New Jersey.

The trip to the Ice House from Great Neck could take as long as an hour and a half. Sarah would have to do her homework in the car. It wouldn't be easy. The question was, would all the effort be worth it?

The answer was yes! All the work and traveling paid off—big time! In 1998, when Sarah was just 12, she skated in the U.S. Junior Figure Skating Championships. *And she won!*

Sarah was definitely a rising star. Everyone was taking notice of her. Reporters were calling. Skating fans began to know her by name.

But there was something all the

Sarah at age 12 skating in the 1998 Junior National Championships in Philadelphia

Sarah with her parents, John and Amy Hughes, after winning the gold medal

judges, reporters and fans didn't know. Sarah's mother was very sick. In fact, she was so sick that she almost didn't get to watch her daughter win at the junior nationals. At the last minute, however, she managed to see her daughter skate one routine.

During her mother's illness, Sarah was probably very sad and afraid. She wanted to be with her mom all the time. But Amy Hughes wanted her daughter to keep on skating.

So Sarah skated. Although her mom couldn't go to all the practices and competitions, she got there when she could. Watching Sarah skate always made her feel better.

Thankfully, Sarah's mom recovered. She made it a point not to miss any more of her daughter's competitions. "After what I went through, I'm going to watch," Amy Hughes told the *New York Daily News*.

And there would be a lot of skating to see. Winning the junior nationals competition was just the beginning of Sarah Hughes's golden journey!

High School–Ice School

Winning the U.S. Junior Championship is a big accomplishment. But it isn't enough to get you into the Olympics. To do that, you have to skate at the senior level, alongside skaters like Michelle Kwan and Irina Slutskaya. If Sarah wanted to fulfill her dreams, she'd have to compete against serious professionals.

In 1999, Sarah made it to the senior

level. She placed fourth at her first U.S. Figure Skating Championships. Then it was on to the World Figure Skating Championships, in Helsinki, Finland, where she placed seventh. Sarah was on her way to reaching her Olympic dream.

Many kids who dream of being Olympic skaters often leave home to live near their coaches. They stay with host families and do little more than work on their skating all day long. Their only schooling is a few hours each week spent with tutors. The only friends they have are other skaters.

But Sarah had no desire to leave home. "Even if I don't make it, I'll have given it my best, and I'll have been around my family," Sarah told a reporter in 1999. "If I went somewhere else, I'd have to live with someone else's family."

Sarah performing at the World Figure Skating
Championships in Helsinki in 1999

Sarah also wasn't giving up on getting a good education. For her, doing well on her schoolwork was every bit as important as landing a perfect triple jump.

Sarah's teachers at Great Neck North High School were eager to help Sarah in any way they could. They understood that Sarah couldn't always be in school, especially since some of her competitions would take her far away to countries like Hungary, France, and Germany. They came up with a way for Sarah to do her schoolwork on the road.

E-mail and cell phones were a big help. Sarah could get her assignments from her teachers by phone, and then e-mail her homework to school. When Sarah wasn't traveling, her teachers would sometimes come to her house and give her a private lesson.

But don't fool yourself. Sarah didn't have it easy just because she wasn't in school all day. In fact, Sarah thought her way of going to school was much tougher.

"One on one it's harder," she told *Newsday*. "You kind of have to do your work."

All of Sarah's hard work really paid off. During her freshman year in high school, she was given the Presidential Award for Academic Excellence. That award is given only to the top students in the country.

Keeping up with her high-school friends is important to Sarah, too, especially now. Although she has very little free time, she makes it a point to stay in touch with the kids at Great Neck North High School. When she's home, she loves hanging out with her old friends and listening to Celine Dion, 'N Sync, and Britney Spears on the stereo. She and her friends also like to play tennis and go Rollerblading. And if she's around on a Monday night,

Sarah performing at the U.S. Figure Skating Championships in Cleveland in 2000

Sarah and her sisters get together and watch *7th Heaven* on TV.

"I wouldn't give that up," Sarah told *USA Today*. "We're always laughing because things that only happen to us we see happening to [the characters]."

When Sarah's away on tour, her friends really miss her. Some of those pals held a big party back on Long Island the night Sarah skated her short program at the Olympics. Imagine their surprise when Sarah thanked them—in front of millions of TV viewers!

"Thank you for having a party for me on the short program," she said into the TV cameras. "I heard it was great."

To most people, Sarah Hughes is a championship skater. But to her friends and teachers, she's a great kid who has managed to stay normal even with all her skating.

As Sarah's English teacher told one reporter, "I want so much for the world to see what I see in her."

Life at the Olympics

When Sarah arrived at the Olympics in Salt Lake City on February 7, 2002, she was amazed at how much free stuff an Olympic athlete is given.

"You know those TV shows where they give you a grocery cart and you have so much time to gather up as much stuff as you can?" Robin Wagner asked one reporter. "That's what it was like."

Sarah and Robin were both given Olympic shirts, jackets, hats, and gloves.

They also got to order special Olympic rings that only athletes and their coaches can get. Then they were treated to a delicious meal at a local restaurant. Everywhere they went, reporters and photographers were right there beside them.

The American Olympic Team at the opening ceremonies

Later that evening, Sarah marched with the U.S. team during the opening ceremonies. *She was one of them. She was an Olympian!*

But before Sarah could get too comfortable with all the fancy meals, free gifts, and flashbulbs, Robin Wagner put her on a plane bound for Colorado Springs. That's where Sarah would be training for the next week. In Colorado Springs there would be no reporters and no other skaters to distract her. There, Sarah could really work.

And Sarah had plenty of work to do. She was an underdog at the Olympics. There was no guarantee that she would win a medal. Of all the American skaters, Sarah was the team's lowest-ranked member. Michelle Kwan had won the 2001 senior nationals. That made her the highest-ranked U.S. team member. Sasha Cohen was the second highest in rank. And Sarah had finished third.

Her American teammates weren't Sarah's only competition. The Russian champion, Irina Slutskaya, would also be skating at the Olympics. Irina was every bit as determined to go for the gold as the American girls were.

Still, no one was counting Sarah out—least of all Sarah herself. She was determined to skate her best in the Olympics. Every day, she practiced from early morning until night. She did her jumps over and over again, making sure that her landings were perfect. She worked on her spins until she was dizzy. She even practiced smiling.

Finally, on Tuesday, February 19, Sarah got the chance to live her dream of skating in the Olympics. Sarah was the fifth out of 27 skaters to skate in the short program. When she skated into the center ice to begin her routine, the crowd cheered wildly.

"I've never had a crowd get that

enthusiastic about me," she told a reporter for *Newsday*.

Sarah skated to the music of "Ave Maria." She did a great job, but it wasn't a perfect skate. "I almost hit the boards on my triple Lutz-double loop combination," Sarah admitted later. "But I didn't touch. I did all my elements."

Sarah performing her short program at the Salt Lake Ice Center

Russian Maria Butyrskaya (left) and Americans Sarah
Hughes (center) and Michelle Kwan (right) waiting
expectantly to take the ice

Sarah finished the short program in
fourth place behind Michelle Kwan, Irina
Slutskaya, and American Sasha Cohen.
That was good enough to allow her to
skate in the long program.

Coming in fourth was actually a good
thing for Sarah. She always skated better

when she's the underdog. "Sarah is better as the chaser than the one being chased," Robin Wagner explained to MSNBC.com.

But Sarah would have to wait two days until she could start chasing. The long program wasn't going to take place until Thursday night.

The night before the long program, Sarah slept in her lucky T-shirt. It's the one with a picture of former Olympic skater Peggy Fleming on it.

"I always wear it to bed the night before I compete," Sarah told a reporter for the *Kansas City Star*.

The lucky T-shirt must have worked. By now, everyone in the world knows what happened the night of Sarah's long program. Sarah took to the ice and skated like she'd never skated before. And in the end, Sarah's best was good enough. She was the golden girl of the 2002 Olympics. As happy as she was for herself, Sarah knew that her teammate Michelle Kwan had taken a big loss. Michelle had placed third, behind Irina Slutskaya, who had come in second.

Michelle had come to the 1998 Olympic Games hoping to bring home the gold. But that medal had gone to American Tara Lipinski. Michelle went home with the second-place silver medal.

Now, she was going home with the third-place bronze. But to Sarah, Michelle was still a winner. "Michelle has always been an idol for me," she told reporters. "Now more than ever. I hope my career will be as bright as hers."

With Sarah skating at her best, and all of America in love with her, it seems that dream will come true as well.

What's Next?

What do you do after you've won an Olympic gold medal? Some Olympic skating champs, like Tara Lipinski, decide to stop competing. They perform in ice shows instead. But that's not what Sarah wanted to do. "I started skating because I love to skate," she told a writer for the Associated Press. "And I started competing because I love to compete. I don't have any plans right now to stop."

Right after the 2002 Olympics, Sarah planned to fly to Japan in March. She wanted to compete in the World Championships in Nagano.

However, Sarah later changed her mind about competing. "Unfortunately, while the past two weeks have been terrific, they have also been exhausting and have not afforded me the opportunity to properly prepare for the competition," Sarah said in a statement.

If Sarah thought her life was busy before the Olympics, she hadn't seen anything yet. The night she won the gold medal she got only two hours of sleep. Then she had to wake up to be interviewed for the *Today Show*. Later, she talked to reporters from all over the world. In between, she spent time with her family.

Sarah was glad to "have a few laughs with my brothers and my sisters...I think they were more interested in the medal than in me," she teased. "I haven't seen them in so long, and they all were saying, 'Where's the medal? Where's the medal?'"

The extra hard work didn't stop after the Olympic closing ceremonies. When someone becomes as famous as Sarah had, lots of companies want him or her to do commercials. Sarah had to decide which companies she wanted to work with. Some people thought Sarah could earn as much as three to five million dollars a year making commercials and personal appearances.

A few days after the Olympics, it was announced that Sarah's picture would appear on boxes of the cereal Wheaties.

"Winning a gold medal is something

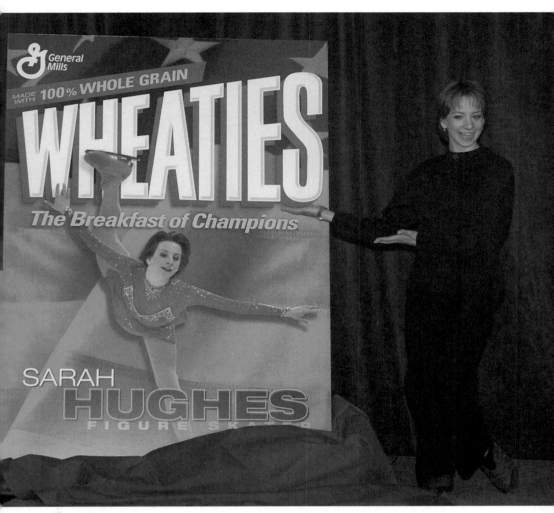

Sarah unveils her Wheaties box at a press conference in Salt Lake City

I've dreamed about for most of my life," Sarah told reporters. "To top it off, now I have my own Wheaties box. This is really a dream come true."

She next flew to Los Angeles to join the Backstreet Boys onstage at the Grammy Awards. Sarah didn't sing with the Boys; she just presented an award.

Later that week, Sarah flew back to New York. She was honored by the New York Rangers hockey team. The town of Great Neck also planned a huge parade in her honor, and declared March 3 Sarah Hughes Day. (The parade was delayed until March 10, though, because of rain.) She even was given the key to New York City by Mayor Michael Bloomberg. Wheaties, Grammys, and parades. Talk about exciting!

Of course, Sarah still has to fit schoolwork into her even busier life. This year, that's especially important. Sarah is studying to take her college entrance exams. Her dream is to go to an Ivy

League school and someday become a doctor.

On top of all that, Sarah's getting ready to take her driving test. When she gets her license, she can drive herself to the Ice House.

No matter what the future holds for Sarah, one thing is for sure. For the rest of her life, she will be known as Olympic Gold Medalist Sarah Hughes. It doesn't get much better than that!

Figure Skating Words

Axel: A jump where the skater takes off on the outside edge of the forward foot and lands on the outside edge of her other foot.

Camel: A spin done on one leg while the other leg is extended straight out in the air.

Crossover: A way to turn corners and pick up speed. The skater crosses one foot over the other.

Edge: Each skate blade has two edges, one on each side. They are called the inside and the outside edge. Each edge is split into two sections, forward and back.

Flip: A jump that is made with the help of the teeth at the front of the skate blade (called the toe-pick). The skater takes off from the back inside edge of one foot and lands on the back outside edge of the other foot.

Lutz: A jump where the skater is moving in a backward curve. She uses her toe to turn in the opposite direction. She takes off from a back outside edge, then lands on the other skate's back outside edge.

Salchow: A jump in which the skater takes off from the back inside edge of one foot and lands backwards on the back outside edge of the other foot.

Toe Loop: A jump where the skater takes off from the back outside edge, spins once, and lands on the same edge.

Competitive Highlights

Year	Competition	Location	Place
2002	Olympic Winter Games	Salt Lake City	1st
2002	US National Figure Skating Championships	Los Angeles	3rd
2002	ISU Grand Prix Final	Kitchener, Ontario, Canada	3rd
2002	Hershey's Kisses Challenge (team)	Auburn Hills, MI	2nd
2001	Trophée Lalique	Paris	2nd
2001	Skate Canada	Saskatoon, Canada	1st
2001	Skate America	Colorado Springs	2nd
2001	World Figure Skating Championships	Vancouver, Canada	3rd
2001	ISU Grand Prix Final	Kitchener, Ontario, Canada	3rd
2001	US National Figure Skating Championships	Boston	2nd
2001	Cup of Russia	St. Petersburg	2nd
2001	Nations Cup	Gelsenkirchen, Germany	3rd
2000	Skate America	Colorado Springs	2nd
2000	International Figure Skating Challenge (team)	Binghamton, NY	2nd
2000	World Figure Skating Championships	Nice, France	5th
2000	US National Figure Skating Championships	Cleveland, OH	5th
2000	Keri Lotion USA vs. World (team)	Orlando, FL	3rd
2000	Trophée Lalique	Paris	1st
2000	Skate America	Colorado Springs	3rd
1999	Vienna Cup	Vienna, Austria	1st
1999	Keri Lotion Classic (Team USA)	Orlando, FL	1st
1999	Hershey's Kisses Challenge (team)	Binghamton, NY	2nd
1999	World Figure Skating Championships	Helsinki	2nd
1999	Junior Grand Prix	Detroit, MI	7th
1999	US National Figure Skating Championships	Salt Lake City	2nd
1999	World Junior Championships	Zagreb, Croatia	2nd
1998	Hungarian Trophy	Budapest	2nd
1998	Mexico Cup	Mexico City	2nd
1998	US Junior Championships	Philadelphia	1st